M000236154

Paws of Love

Transforming Grief to Empowerment:

7 Spiritual Practices

FIRST EDITION:
ttlharmony Publishing

ttlharmony
PUBLISHING

www.ttlharmonyPublishing.com www.yourdivineplan.net

Publisher's Cataloging-In-Publication Data
(Prepared by The Donohue Group, Inc.)

Names: Ishwari, author.
Title: Paws of love : transforming grief to empowerment :
7 spiritual practices / Ishwari (Rina Lichtinger).
Description: First edition. | [Candler, North Carolina] :
ttlharmony Publishing, [2020] | Includes bibliographical
references and index.
Identifiers: ISBN 9781736290101 (paperback) | ISBN
9781736290118 (ebook)
Subjects: LCSH: Ishwari—Psychology. | Dog owners—
Psychology. | Dogs—Death—Psychological aspects. |
Grief. | Spiritual exercises.
Classification: LCC SF422.86 .I89 2020 (print) | LCC
SF422.86 (ebook) | DDC 636.70887—dc23

Printed in the United States of America

Paws of Love

Transforming Grief to Empowerment:
7 Spiritual Practices

Ishwari *(Rina Lichtinger)*

Praise for Paws of Love

"*Paws of Love* is a heartwarming healing book and a must read for every dog lover. Ishwari's intimate spiritual journey with her dog Rexi deeply touched my soul. The 7 spiritual practices gracefully walk a griever through a healing of the body, heart and mind."

—**Wendy Wennberg,** MBA, ACC, NLP, Certified Advanced Grief Recovery Specialist

"*Paws of Love* is a beautiful story about the love between two souls—a human and a dog. The bond between them is so eloquently written. The love and grief Ishwari has for Rexi jumped from the page. Her steps used through the grieving process provide a personal view into her own healing and provide others with a simple-to-follow guideline to help them on their journeys. I highly recommend this book for those who are experiencing the deep loss of a pet and desire to learn of

ways to cope and move through grief into a place of peace."
—**Charlene Christiano**, ANP-BC, Integrative Health Practitioner

"*Paws of Love* is the best book ever written about losing a dog and how to listen to God and transform the unbearable into something positive. Ishwari gifts the world with a clear roadmap for how to do this, while interweaving her own intimate and amazing journey."
—**Natalia Morales**, Owner of Lollipaws Grooming Services

"The degree to which our pets can touch our hearts and impact our lives is astonishing. To participate in that bond is a blessing and privilege. Thank you, Rexi and Ishwari."
—**Douglas Thieme,** DVM, Seiler Animal Hospital

"I fell in love with Rexi. And, with Ishwari too! Thank you for this gift to the world. In this time of uncertainty, *Paws of Love* helped me open my heart and know unseen worlds are indeed real. My heart is opening to joy and hope for how our world may ascend and have humanity evolve to a higher vibration place of unconditional love and light."

—**Margot Gobetti,** MD, Homeopathy & Anthroposophic Medicine, Holistic Healer

"I absolutely loved *Paws of Love*. As someone who works with dogs for a living, I spend all day witnessing the amazing relationship between dogs and their humans. And as a lifelong caretaker of my own dogs, I've experienced firsthand the joy and comfort that they have brought into my life, as well as the grief and sorrow at their eventual passing.

I've been privileged to see Ishwari's relationship with her current Frenchie, Magu, in a close-up and personal way. Her love is so apparent and radiates from her during every interaction with the little bundle of unbridled energy.

Ishwari's book, based on her own experiences with her beloved furry companions, is a beautifully written, easily understandable explanation of the grieving and healing process. She offers clear, compassionate guidance on how to deal with emotional pain, helping the reader back to a place of peace, joy and acceptance.

I'd recommend *Paws of Love* to all animal lovers, and particularly to anyone suffering the loss of a beloved companion."
   —**Jason Woodle**, Owner, Dogtopia of Fort Lauderdale—Northeast

"I have been privileged to know and experience the healing energy and love of Rexi. Ishwari's book teaches us much more than how to heal from the loss of a pet—it is a manual for grieving loss of any kind—human as well as canine (or feline in my case!) Most importantly it teaches us that grief is an individual process and that we must honor that process in ourselves and others. I really love this book."

—**Marcia A Gill**, RN, CHTP, Energy Healer

"Every so often a person comes into your life that you recognize at a deeper level of consciousness. Ishwari is one of those amazing souls, and we became friends immediately twenty-one years ago. I have continued to watch her grow into an exceptional spiritual leader. I LOVE *Paws of Love*. It is clear and yet deeply moving regarding all our relationships in life. I had the pleasure of knowing Rexi and witnessing the beautiful bond between them. I definitely think even people who haven't lost a dog will find this book a joy to read and inspiring."

—**Nancy L. Wingerter**, Publisher/Author of *Wisdom of the Soul*, Instructor for over twenty years in Vibrational Healing, Holistic Nurse, Speaker

"*Paws of Love* is an extremely enjoyable book that takes by the hand any person who has experienced grief because of the loss of their beloved dog companion. Ishwari takes us into a journey of emotions, helping us to acknowledge and recognize the emotions and pain that go deeply into the soul. She shows us the possibility of finding the inner and outer light. The "7 lessons" are helpful to follow and a great guide. I really enjoyed the order in which the processing will unfold for those who read this beautiful book. Thank you, Ishwari."

—**Arlette Rothhirsch**, D.V.M., M.D., veterinarian, former surgeon, animal communicator, energy healer, human consciousness teacher, and the author of seven published books

"The Seven Spiritual Practices in *Paws of Love* provide a blueprint for not only how to recover from grief with dog loss, but also how to thrive spiritually in this challenging, transitional epoch of human history we are living in. Ishwari is a true healer and a gift to humanity."

—**Sherine Bichara**, Owner of Elixir of Life by L'Alchimiste

"This book is about how to heal and move through grief after the physical loss of a beloved pet. However, it's much broader than that. Maybe a bit like the classic, *Jonathan Livingston Seagull*. It is also a beautiful and inspiring story about life, spirituality and the afterlife. I love this book. Best ever!"

—**Sharon Gruber**, RN, LMT, HT practitioner & energy therapist

"I devoured this wonderful book about the passing of our pets and emotional guardians! It brought tears of joy to me. Ishwari takes us through the five stages of grief—denial, anger, bargaining, sadness and acceptance. She shares with us how a strong spiritual practice and the connection to source got her through the darkest hours as she realized the only constant one must accept is change. This book is a must read for all pet owners. I wish I had these lessons shared with me when I lost my companion, Jabulani."

—**Elsa Maldonado**, Forever Student, Forever Teacher and Owner of Pawfidant

"Ishwari was able to express exactly the feelings and the spiritual connections we have with our fur babies. I've known Ishwari for many years and she is an inspiration to many souls. I related to her expressions of Love Lost but yet not far away. Anyone who has a fur baby should read about her journey through this expression of pure Love."

—**Dr. and Rev. Peg Gordon**, *DDMS, mentor of Alliance of Divine Love doctoral program*

"Ishwari shares in a very beautiful way her recovery from grief over the loss of her beloved Rexi. Her feelings are so real and so well explained that we can follow her transformation and relate it to our own journey with grief. *Paws of Love* reinforces our inner knowingness that we shouldn't be afraid to feel our emotions as we go through the stages of grieving. I recommend this book not only for people who have lost a beloved animal, but for anybody who experiences a loss. Thank you, Ishwari, for reinforcing our inner knowingness that learning how to live and enjoy life again is the best present we can give our beloved who left us in the material world."

—**Ruth Chayet**, M.A. in Learning Disabilities and Family Therapy, parent consultation and course facilitator Neufield Institute, Creator of *"Love Coaching"*

"Thank you, Ishwari, for a very beautiful and profound book. I cried a couple of times while advancing through the chapters, for I also went through a loss of a beloved animal. In 2013, my cat Morpheus died, and I have never cried so much in my life. He was an amazing and beautiful cat, and a teacher and a healer in my life. I adored him and he adored me. I completely relate to everything you went through. After Morpheus passed, he visited me on many nights to let me know that we never die but live in the spirit realm after this lifetime. I love this book and I know that it will help a lot of people going through the grieving process after losing an animal that is part of their heart and soul."

—**Grace Terry**, Founder of the Infinite Voice Academy, soul singer, producer, composer and sound healer

"Ishwari has so gracefully and inspiringly drawn upon lifetimes of sacred wisdom to transmute the pain of grief and write this book. It is a gift to anyone coping with the loss of a four-legged (or any, really) loved one and a true testament to how suffering can bring us closer to great Love and great Beauty. And oh, how I fell in love with Rexi over and over while reading the stories about him Ishwari has woven into this gem!"

—**Nasim Sattar,** CPA and 300 Hour Certified Hatha Yoga Teacher

"Ishwari's story of her journey with her beloved Rexi is inspiring. I recommend *Paws of Love* to anyone on a spiritual journey, and to those who seek comfort after their beloved pet has gone on to pure source. A beautiful read."

—**Richard Wexler**, yogi, barber, massage therapist

"This beautiful book is for everyone who loses their fur-baby. As an animal advocate and dog salon owner, I understand the death of a dog is devastating to many and creates the same or more pain as losing a human loved one. Ishwari will guide you through the darkness of loss to reach inner peace and healing."

—**Danielle Gaudreau**, Animal advocate and Salon Bark Spa and Boutique owner

"I love this book! It is admirable that Rina had the courage to express such deep intimate emotions. The average person just keeps it in. I was inspired with the way Ishwari unites humans and animals in a unique bond."

—**Theresa Waisman**, Ph.D., Political Philosophy (Sorbonne University) and Literature (Autonomous National University of Mexico (UNAM)), over forty years as Professor of Literature and Philosophy, UNAM, and author of *Modernization of Mexico*

"Without love we wouldn't have grief. Ishwari shares her amazing story and gives a path for healing from the loss of a beloved pet."
—**Lana Medford**, retired teacher, Cabarrus County Schools: Harrisburg, North Carolina

"Grief over the loss of a loved one can be devastating. For some it hits just as hard when it is a pet. Ishwari recounts the prolonged agony of losing her beloved French bulldog Rexi. This led her to seek solace through a variety of spiritual practices and beliefs that included meditation, the practice of gratitude, and the channeling of her pet from "the other side." She's led finally to peace and shares a bundle of steps that those in similar distress could profit by."
—**John R. Dolen**, writer, editor, journalist

"What a beautiful book. Love it! I believe it will help a lot of people. I learned very much about grieving when I lost my parents at a very young age. Grieving over the loss of a pet is a very personal experience that sometimes others don't understand."

—**Julio Lacayo**, Owner, 305 Doggie

Contents

Foreword xxi

Dedication...xxix

My Beloved Rexi 1

Dogs Are the Healers of Society.............. 11

Rocky: Eight Years of Love 17

The 7 Spiritual Practices: 21

Spiritual Practice #1:....................................23

Spiritual Practice #2:....................................29

Spiritual Practice #3:....................................47

Spiritual Practice #4:....................................59

Spiritual Practice #5:....................................71

Spiritual Practice #6:....................................77

Spiritual Practice #7:....................................99

Acknowledgments.................................... 115

About the Author...................................... 117

Foreword

Have you ever wondered what your soul really is, or whether the various animals on Earth have souls as well? Do our favorite departed dogs live on with us when we leave our earthly bodies?

I used to think about these very questions even when I was a young child. When I read the manuscript for this beautiful book by Ishwari, similar thoughts returned from so many years ago. Ishwari has created in *Paws of Love* a truly profound book of spiritual guidance on the concept of the soul and how it relates to us as humans and to our beloved animals. I sense that her spiritual teachers and the Ascended Masters in the higher realms were instrumental in bringing the Divine light of this book's core truth to her and through her—and out to you, dear readers. These lessons can lay or strengthen the foundation for a strong spiritual life. Build with these lessons a new life of understanding and you will be building "a house upon a rock."

In 2007, a strange and mystical "presence" moved me out of my house and into my car. I had a sudden but peaceful awareness that I needed to make the fifteen-minute drive to a metaphysical church in a near-by town. That experience opened doors I believed only existed in legends and movies.

I later learned through "spirit communication" that the soul consciousness of a dying minister at that little church was the same "mystical presence" that inspired my short road trip. Her goal was to enable me to continue her ministry while unfolding my own latent and yet-to-be-discovered gifts of the Spirit. Looking back, I was being prepared years ago for the incredible public-speaking ministry and coaching career I have today.

Not long after joining that metaphysical church, I came across an advertisement by Ishwari offering Reiki healing sessions and spiritual classes. I remember feeling a strong sense of "needing" to make an appointment soon, so I did so right away and now I can see how important that encounter was for my new spiritual beginnings. Today, we call this an "awakening of consciousness" in our life path and purpose.

My reason for seeking out Ishwari all those years ago was to seek healing for chronic pain and to also begin learning about chakras, meditation and all things metaphysical. I can still recall how much pain relief and peace I experienced during that first session and for several days that followed. I was surprised someone mystical like her, who was using techniques that seemed strange to me at that time and I didn't fully understand or believe in, could be of help to me so easily. She unknowingly would help change my perspective on such mystical realities.

Ishwari's loving and nurturing nature was deeply needed by my heart and my soul, and especially the little immature unspiritual me. The lotus seed of me simply existed in its earthly muddy waters, unaware of what lay dormant in my own potential and the magnificence of what existed beyond the surface waters of this life. Ishwari's spiritual gifts profoundly touched my own spirit, bringing me hope, inspiration and joy that I had lacked for years in my search for a better life on Earth.

Ishwari's ministry and healing stoked the flames in my soul's desires. I began to seek out other "metaphysical waters" of knowledge, teachers, experiences and even my own potential spiritual gifts. Within a couple of years, I became well-known in our community as a supporter and host to numerous presenters offering esoteric topics and modalities within metaphysics, Eastern traditions, Native American traditions and the mystical branches of various world religions. At the peak of my ministry, I became the leader of the largest and most successful metaphysical center and church in Florida—the Metaphysical Chapel of South Florida. I brought in healers, intuitives and mediums from around the globe to demonstrate their spiritual gifts and to teach my community of the incredible, powerful and beautiful abilities and potential within every human soul. Our community learned not only how to unfold those spiritual faculties but also how to use them for discovering their Divine Purpose in life.

I can say unequivocally that this is no ordinary book on the love we have for our beloved animals, even after they make their transition. *Paws of Love* is a book of inspiration, hope, encouragement, possibilities, and of love as expressed between the souls—humans and their non-human beloved family members.

So few books speak of the body, mind, and spirit principles in relation to us and our dogs or cats, especially to the dying experience and the soul's existence in the afterlife. This book is a rare gift to us all because *Paws of Love* is the flow of Spirit to Ishwari, through Ishwari, and back out to the Universe—a great Divine Circle of Love! Indeed, this book is the Universal Law of Love in motion.

Spirit has often told me how every soul that comes to this material dimension of existence is given a human body temple suited to their purpose. Why is this so important to share? Because I want others to realize how incredibly rare and special their soul faculty is in our universe. My greatest wish for you, dear reader, is that the light of higher truth found in the profound pages of Ishwari's powerful book nourishes and awakens a new understanding, not only of your soul's journey, but of the Divine connections we create with our precious and beloved animals.

—**Kevin Lee**, International Bestselling Author (*Your Divine Purpose: A Journey to Fulfillment and Legacy*), Conscious Business Coach and Motivational Speaker. www.RevKevinLee.com

Dedication

To Rexi-ji, my beloved French bulldog and healing partner. For twelve wonderful years, we loved, played and found joy together as he taught me how to get in touch with my inner child.

My Beloved Rexi

His name was Rexi, but I often called him Rexi-ji because I'm drawn to many of the spiritual practices of India, where people sometimes add the suffix "ji" to a saintly person's name.

Rexi was a French bulldog, not a person, yet within him dwelled the wisdom, love and compassion of a great yogi, so I felt in my heart that I should call him Rexi-ji.

He had the potential of a show dog, with a sturdy frame and perfectly proportioned, muscular body; large, pointy ears; a beautiful fawn-white coat; and a perpetual smile on his rugged face. He was a bit of a showoff around other dogs, strutting like a king and making sure he was the center of attention. Yes, everyone noticed him.

French bulldogs, or "Frenchies," have a unique puppy-like cry, and Rexi's sounded a bit like "mama." But it was a happy cry, not lonely or plaintive, for he had a curiosity for life and a special love for people.

Rexi weighed a healthy thirty-five pounds, so he was larger than most French bulldogs. When he played at the dog park, he'd sometimes try to gently intimidate smaller dogs but fit in with larger dogs and become part of their "pack." He'd mark his territory and jump in and out of the water and onto tiny rafts, happy to romp with his doggie friends.

Rexi loved nature, especially the heavily wooded Hugh Taylor Birch State Park, next to Fort Lauderdale's world-famous beach on the Atlantic Ocean. He'd sniff the many smells, investigate the texture of the grass, and perk up his ears at the sounds of nature.

When we arrived at the park, he'd squeal and strain at his leash as we got out of the car. Sometimes a friendly park ranger would give him treats. He loved the park so much, I made it a New Year's resolution to take him there every week.

Rexi also enjoyed going to the ocean at night, when spiritual groups met on the beach to play Tibetan singing bowls and chant mantras and hymns from the Vedic, Hindu tradition. He connected with calm music, yoga, and all kinds of smells, including Palo Santo incense, the "holy stick" used for centuries in cleansing and purifying rituals by the indigenous people of the Andes.

At home, when he wasn't curled up in a soft blanket, he loved playing with the water hose at bathing time or watching me swim laps in the pool. Sometimes I would splash water towards him and he would try to catch it in his mouth. He would join me, too, at the Jacuzzi, lying outside the tub while placing his front paws in the warm water.

Rexi loved foods like jicama, carrots, cucumber, watermelon, cheese, and fresh-baked bread with olive oil. Yet, like most dogs, he also loved meat. He especially savored the big bones we'd give him after family gatherings when my son, Alexis, grilled steaks. I didn't share in this part of the meal, because I generally prefer to be nourished with a plant-based diet. Rexi, on the other hand, would go crazy over the smell and flavor of the meat.

Rexi was neutered as a puppy, but after every meal he would grab and hump his bed. It was his thing, and I could tell he thought it was funny. I'm sure that if you've ever had a puppy, you're familiar with this type of behavior.

I work as a spiritual healer, and some of my clients also become close friends. Among them was Patty, who, with her husband, moved from Los Angeles to Fort Lauderdale for retirement. In her early 60s, she was thin with gorgeous blonde hair and deep-set blue eyes. Patty was quite beautiful on the outside, but her true beauty came from within.

As soon as we met, there was a deep connection. I felt that I knew Patty, and that we were kindred spirits on the same spiritual path.

For two years, Patty came to me regularly for Reiki treatments and healing touch. She participated in meditations when I played Tibetan singing bowls. She also took many of the workshops I offered and came each month to a shamanic ceremony and meditation that I held in my home.

During the meditations, Rexi always sought to be near her. It was as if he felt the same kindred connection to Patty as I did.

The last workshop she attended included an Inca Medicine Wheel initiation. This initiation connects the physical and spiritual worlds. During this profound healing process, some participants experience higher realms of consciousness and have their psychic powers awakened.

Afterwards, Patty told me, "I am at peace. I don't know what I saw and felt, but it was Divine. I was 'home' and I didn't want to come back." No doubt she had experienced what existence is like in the afterlife.

Not long after that, Patty mentioned to me that something was going on with her liver and she would be seeing another doctor for a second opinion. A week later I visited her in a hospital where she was dying of advanced liver cancer.

I did what I could to ease her discomfort with hands-on healing. I also anointed her feet and forehead with an aromatherapy blend I made based on a practice from ancient Egypt that included the hallowed ingredients sandalwood and frankincense. I saw a tunnel of light and knew it was time for her to go to the light, enveloped in peace and love. Patty fell asleep peacefully, and I left knowing this would be my final goodbye.

The next day, Patty's daughter called to tell me her mother had crossed over. For days I could still feel Patty's presence and sense her beautiful smile.

The next time the group met, Rexi immediately sat on the floor at the place in the circle where Patty used to sit. All of us looked at each other in amazement. We knew Patty was with us, and we acknowledged her presence with a prayer.

Rexi, my beloved friend and companion, didn't stir. He lay in Patty's spot and slept peacefully for the entire two hours of the workshop. I believe Rexi could see Patty and connect telepathically with her soul.

Animals, like humans, have choices to reincarnate for a purpose. Rexi chose to come into my circle of relatives and friends who were yogis, meditators, and healers.

He came in doggie form as a teacher for all of us. He taught me how to nurture my inner child, and showed everyone how to begin and end a day with a grateful heart. Rexi came on four legs to bring healing love to all aspects of humanity. This was his essence, and he left his loving paw prints everywhere he went.

I grieved deeply when Rexi passed from the material world in August 2019. I'm sure many of you know the pain that comes with the loss of a dog you have grown to love with all your heart, and who loves you unconditionally always and forever.

Perhaps that is why you are reading this book. It certainly is the reason I wrote it. In grief, we feel emotions we don't want to feel, but God has reasons for the experiences that cause us so much sorrow. Ultimately, we are able to flow through the devastation of grief—towards empowerment.

Dogs Are the Healers of Society

After Rexi had passed into spirit form, he communicated through thought to me, "Dogs are the healers of society."

A special bond exists between humans and animals who are members of our families. For many people, that bond is strongest with their dogs. When we are with them, we often become silly and childlike. Dogs can act like children, energetic and playful all day long. From the moment we awake until we fall asleep, our lives gravitate towards our dogs.

We walk them, feed them, play and cuddle with them. They are always super attuned to our feelings, for our hearts are always connected. For many of us, these angels are our children, partners and best pals. They ask for nothing from us, yet faithfully watch over us and give us love.

When something changes emotionally or physically in people's lives, dogs perceive this, and it affects the way they act. They might stay very close to their human and insist that they be held in his or her lap. This causes a shift of energy in the human.

When a human's energy is out of balance, whether through a life pattern or a short-term choice of behavior, our doggie angels respond. For instance, if a spouse or child is on a cell phone during dinner, ignoring other members of the family, a dog might bring attention to this less-than-ideal behavior by yapping or barking. Once the cell phone is set aside and the family engages in conversation, the perceptive dog will settle right down.

Can we make sense of the connections we have with these beings of another species who live with us? Why do we love them so deeply? Why do they mean so much to us?

It's common to hear people address these oft-unspoken questions by saying we love our dogs so much because they love us unconditionally. In my heart, I know that's true. The essence of unconditional love is formless and unlimited. It is the strongest bond in the Universe, and a dog without hesitation will sacrifice his or her own life to protect the life of a human it loves who is faced with danger.

But sometimes I wonder, *Is there something besides unconditional love in this magical dynamic?*

Have you ever wondered why you select a certain puppy from a pet store or a breeder, or adopt one dog rather than another from an animal shelter? Have you ever considered whether a spiritual bond between you and your dog stems from past lives spent together on Earth, or as spirit beings in another realm? Have we and our dogs agreed to incarnate together on Planet Earth, perhaps for many lifetimes? Have our dogs shown up in our current lifetimes to emotionally support and protect us, and teach us lessons we need to learn? I think so, and we'll explore these questions in the upcoming chapters.

Our animal family members certainly have a close connection with spiritual realms. When I did hands-on healing with clients with Rexi in the room, he would gaze at a particular spot without moving or barking. I knew he could see, hear and feel a spiritual presence in the same way that I, as a clairvoyant, can see spiritual signs.

Our society is not sensitive enough at this point to recognize our beloved animals as equals to humans, so people often lack sufficient empathy and compassion when others experience the death of a beloved non-human family member. They don't realize that a person's grief can be as deep as, or in some cases even deeper than, when they lose a human loved one.

Sometimes coping with the loss can be even more difficult because our dogs, in a sense, are our emotional guardians and, for many of us, our constant companions. They sense our every feeling, send us healing energy when we need it, and share their love, playfulness and joy with us. Our dogs always love and forgive us—always.

Some people, well-meaning perhaps, may tell you that the best way to cope with the loss of a beloved dog is to get another one right away, as if they were replaceable parts in a machine. That may help some people cope with grief, but certainly not all, or even most. Grief takes time to process, and the biggest mistake a person can make is to try to cover it up. Your dog dwells in the spiritual realm, in happiness. The one left behind in sadness is you.

Rocky: Eight Years of Love

Before Rexi, my family and I were blessed to have Rocky. He also was a beautiful French bulldog. Rocky was in good health, although sometimes in Florida's hot and humid summers he would tire during his daily walk and I would have to carry him home.

When he was eight years old, however, Rocky came down with what seemed to be a cold. We went back and forth to the veterinarian, who finally felt it necessary to keep Rocky for a week to give him strong antibiotics and intravenous treatments.

I visited Rocky at the vet's office. He had an IV in his paw, and when he looked at me, he seemed so sad. I connected intuitively with him, and he seemed to say, "my heart." I asked the veterinarian whether Rocky had heart problems, and he told me the problem was strictly with his lungs

I had to leave town for a few days and was shocked when my husband called to tell me Rocky had deteriorated rapidly and the vet had recommended he be put to sleep. My husband stayed with Rocky until the end.

Because Rocky died when I was away, I had no closure. Sadness consumed me. I became numb, and nothing and no one could make me feel whole again.

When I returned home, I compiled a photo album with pictures of Rocky. I also placed his ashes on the altar of a Buddhist center I attended, and the members and I prayed for Rocky's transcendence. The members of the center also provided me with much-needed emotional support.

I wondered, too, whether the "my heart" message I received from Rocky the last time I was with him had a special meaning, so I asked an animal communicator to try to channel a message from Rocky. I was astonished when I received the email response from him, in which Rocky said:

"I am eternal. I love you so much. I couldn't fit in this small body, my energy body is just so much bigger than this physical form. Yes, I was saying goodbye when you heard me say 'my heart.' I am happy you paid attention. I have deeper spiritual work from the other side. I completed my life happy and loved. I know I will always be in your hearts."

My heart skipped a beat when I read the ending of the channeled message, which confirmed that Rocky was communicating from the spirit world: *"I enjoyed the doggie birthday party and wanted more cake. I really liked that!"*

Each year of his life, I would take Rocky to the house of a friend where we would celebrate her poodle's birthday—with a carrot cake made specially for the doggies.

The 7 Spiritual Practices:

Evolving from Grief to Empowerment

Spiritual Practice
#1:

Give yourself permission to grieve deeply in your own way.

Unconditional love is without boundaries, expectations or regrets. When our beloved animals leave us, understandably we experience sadness, fear, and even a sense of abandonment.

Often the first thing we want to do is isolate ourselves, avoiding contact with other people as much as possible. Quiet can be our best friend. The physical body even can react with a loss of appetite and with muscular pain—including pain in the heart.

After my beloved Rexi transitioned, I felt lost, sad, empty, and angry. The days passed as if I were in a fog. I reached inside myself but found I couldn't meditate or concentrate, which always had been part of my daily spiritual practice of connecting with the Divine. My inner world had collapsed, and I found myself in a dark place I had never fully known. I had come face-to-face with my "shadow"—the dark side of the soul.

Yet, as I would learn, every shadow contains a gift.

If you have just lost a beloved animal, you may think you are alone in your sadness and nothing will fill the hole left in your heart. Or, you may try to pretend the roller coaster of emotions you are on is no big deal, although deep within you know this is not so.

All this is understandable, for a best friend and companion has left you. At times you may feel numb. Do the best you can to stay positive. Consider that the numbness you are experiencing is actually an extremely fertile state of awareness that could even change your approach to life.

Rexi's passing caused me to face fears I wasn't even aware I had. To soothe my soul, I embraced the Divine even more tightly as I opened myself to learning more of life's lessons. Recovering from grief is a slow process, but it is one that can lead to harmony, peace of mind, and the true light of empowerment. The emotions of grief are agonizing, but remember, on the other side of the pain is the potential for unbounded spiritual growth.

We must give ourselves permission to grieve in our own ways. Personally, I sought tangible reminders of Rexi's love. I was so sad, I took his blanket and held it tightly as I fell asleep, calling out his name over and over again, trying to feel his soft presence and hear his gentle snoring. Holding onto a beloved animal's belongings is a sign of how greatly you cherished him or her.

I shared pictures of Rexi with friends and found solace in their compassionate reactions to the hurt in my heart. This deepened my bonds with them and helped me recognize that I did not have to go through my suffering alone.

I kept Rexi's bed and favorite toys, washed and stored them, hoping that someday I would be strong enough emotionally to bring a new puppy into my life who would enjoy them as much as Rexi had.

An emotional cord connects you with your beloved animal, who will stay with you in spirit until you decide it's okay for him/her to cross over completely to the celestial realm. After Rexi passed, I could sense his presence through occasional tingling in my body. Sometimes he would appear in a vision and telepathically tell me that he had not left me. If only for that moment, I would feel ecstatic with love.

Through attachment we strive to

compensate for our trauma and sadness. My endless tears were my salvation, and validation of the years of love Rexi and I had shared. In dealing with my grief in my own way, I finally came to understand in the depth of my soul a great spiritual lesson: *The only constant in the Universe is change.*

I am Ishwari, but I am not the same Ishwari as I was when I was a child, or even the same Ishwari as I was yesterday. In the same way, Rexi is not the same Rexi. He still exists, but in a different form.

It took time for me to accept this, but when I did, I could smile again. I still cherish the memories of Rexi, but now know deep in my heart that although the physical form changes and passes on, the spirit never dies.

Spiritual Practice
#2:

Honor the time your soul needs to process grief.

Millions of people throughout the world are familiar with the work of the late psychiatrist Elisabeth Kübler-Ross, who developed the concept of the "Five Stages of Grief." She taught that moving through grief involves a sequence of emotions that build on each other as each of us processes grief in his or her own unique ways.

The first emotion is generally **DENIAL**. We feel stunned and bewildered from the shock of a loved one's dying, and life for us somehow seems unreal. Denial enables us to cope initially with the loss of relatives, friends or beloved animals, and get through the day by letting in only those feelings we can handle.

As denial fades, **ANGER** begins to surface. The grief-stricken person often lashes out at family, friends, themselves, God, the doctor or veterinarian, or the world in general. Many of us have been taught to suppress anger, but it is more healthful to feel it and allow for a process of ultimately releasing the anger. Feeling and processing anger are more constructive than the numbness that accompanies denial. Indeed, anger demonstrates the depth of love one has for the departed.

Many Eastern healing practices assert that disease is caused by blocked energy. Good health, on the other hand, reflects a beautiful, flowing stream of energy. The concept of "that which we resist persists" captures how energy works in our beings. When we allow ourselves to feel our anger, rather than resist it, our energy can again flow unobstructed. This open up the healing process to whatever comes next.

A person suffering from a loss also begins to **BARGAIN**, asking for a deal with God, the veterinarian, or the clergy. Comments such as, "I'll go to church every day, if only my darling will come back to me," are common.

DEPRESSION is a reaction to the changed way of life created by the loss of a loved one. The grieving person may sink into despair, helpless and drained of energy. Some people may think they are mentally ill, but they are not, for depression is a natural response to a momentous loss.

31

The important thing to remember is that the depression will pass, although it can seem that it will last forever.

Finally, **ACCEPTANCE** of the loss begins to surface like the sprout of a plant emerging from the earth. Acceptance does not mean that you have become okay with the loss, but rather that you recognize you must live in a new reality, without the physical presence of the person or beloved animal. When we accept the loss, we can make new connections through which we find joy and happiness. In a sense, we change from a chrysalis into a butterfly as we begin reshaping our lives.

Some people find it healing to believe the Divine had a reason to create this deep experience of loss. I know I did. It seems Rexi's soul was ready to transition into spirit. Maybe I was meant at the time to learn certain things, with Rexi helping me from "across the veil."

Even when devastating events happen, I believe God is always profoundly loving and never punishing. You might even consider the concept, "In all things be grateful." This might be difficult at the time of a shattering loss. I know it was for me. But as I worked my way through the Kübler-Ross stages of grief and evolved to a place of acceptance, I understood that God and Rexi chose the Divine timing for Rexi's transition to spirit. His passing taught me so much, including how to accept myself as I am.

It also showed me what I still needed to accomplish with my life. During the Acceptance stage of grief, I finally became ready to accept the gifts from God that followed the devastating loss of Rexi.

It is important to remember that we are all unique and no one passes through the Five Stages of Grief in a linear way. The feelings associated with the stages may come and go and skip around. In time, however, as we allow our feelings to flow through us, we will process the grief and move on towards a brighter future.

Moving through the Five Stages

The emotions we experience during the five stages can be painful, but everything happens for a reason. None of us would invite pain into our lives, but God, or whatever you choose to call Source, has a broader perspective. By allowing ourselves to process the unwelcome and brutal pain that comes with grief, we open ourselves to the possibility of profound spiritual growth.

Here are some ways I processed my grief. I hope you find them helpful:

- The pain of Rexi's passing caused me to change my perspective. I started focusing not on what I had lost with

Rexi's death, but on all I had gained and learned during the twelve years Rexi and I shared our love while he was with me in physical form.

- I made a point of writing down my feelings in a journal, and reliving and savoring the gifts of joy, patience and caring Rexi had given me. If you have lost a treasured animal, I suggest you consider writing down your feelings and memories, recalling especially all those things you are grateful for. Remember: You did all you could to make your precious animal happy and healthy, and he or she would want you now to find new ways of living with joy.

- For weeks after Rexi's passing I found I could not meditate or perform my daily hatha yoga practice. I did, however, silently chant each night in bed the Sanskrit mantra *Om Namah Shivaya*. It is an Initiation mantra that anyone can chant. Saying it over and over helped settle my mind. This enabled me to fall asleep, and even feel a bit of bliss at times.

The goal of practicing a sacred mantra is to achieve self-realization. When a seeker recites mantra repetitions daily, beautiful life changes can take place as the seeker's energy begins to resonate with the Divine sounds.

The renowned Indian guru Swami Muktananda, who transitioned into spirit in 1982, helped introduce *Om Namah Shivaya* to the West. Om is the primordial sound from which the Universe arose. *Namah* means "to honor." *Shivaya* refers to the deity Shiva, the Supreme Self of all.

More than twenty years ago, I had a deeply personal and profound experience with Muktananda. I had heard of him but had never read any of his books or even known how to spell his name. Yet, he appeared to me in a vivid dream in which he gave me this profound message in English: *"Meditate on your Self. Honor your Self. Worship your Self. Understand your own Self. God dwells within you as you."*

Muktananda's words validated my spiritual practices—and everything I had come to believe.

I suggest you try chanting this or another mantra, or a prayer from a tradition with which you are comfortable.

- Gradually I was drawn to play my Tibetan singing bowls, the sounds of which resonate with my soul and are a source of soothing comfort for me. In the off chance you have some, consider playing them. If not, you might try listening to recordings. The beautiful sound vibrations can reduce stress, physical pain, anxiety, anger, and even blood pressure.

The bowls' resonance also helps balance

the energy centers of the body, known in Eastern spiritual traditions as "chakras," contributing to happiness and well-being. There are a variety of approaches that can be used to balance the chakras, including the energy healing technique Reiki and the placement of crystals at various points on the body. Regardless of the method, when your chakras are balanced you will feel enhanced inner harmony, peace, happiness, and well-being.

- Repeating affirmations helped me get through particularly difficult moments: I am in harmony with my emotions; I am joyful; All is well in my world; I trust the Divine Plan. I also found it useful to take five deep breaths from time to time. This would usually shift my energy in a positive direction. Sometimes when I was feeling particularly sad, I would think about a joyful and playful memory of my beloved Rexi, and that would help me smile from my heart, even if just for a few moments.

- Some people don't want to talk about painful emotions. They try to ignore them, which is the same as burying them deep inside. Talking about your feelings, even when this is painful or uncomfortable, is vital in moving through grief. I encourage you to discuss your feelings with others. You no doubt will find, as I did, that friends and family members really do love you and are more than willing to listen.

- Again, consider that everything is energy and that good health results when our energy flows freely, like a bubbling brook. Talking about your feelings helps that brook continue to flow. By talking, you process your feelings and move through them while honoring the vibrant health of your body.

Eventually I felt good enough to reorganize my home, clean out the drawers and fix up the yard—an acknowledgment that it was time to begin a fresh new phase of my life.

Moving through the Five Stages of Grief requires patience, but also action. When you're in the depths of grief, action may seem impossible, but there will come a time when you feel liberated and energized. Muddled emotions will shift to insight, inspiration, even illumination.

Have faith, nurture yourself, accept your imperfections. Most of all, learn to love yourself as much as your beloved animal loves you.

Euthanasia

Some dogs pass away suddenly, but most do not, and a time will come when signs appear that their lives are ebbing quickly. They may lose control of their bowels or bladders, lose their appetites, ignore their favorite toys, and be so fatigued they can barely move.

As our animal family members draw closer to death, they may seem to lose interest in the people around them. This doesn't mean they don't still care. Their love has not faded; they just don't have the energy to show it in the familiar way.

Some people cannot bring themselves to have a veterinarian intervene and compassionately assist with the passing. This is understandable because we live in a society where it is generally unacceptable to facilitate the transition process for humans.

Some people may not be able to bear the thought of losing their four-legged companion, or perhaps they have the spiritual belief that it is not for them to choose the timing of their dog's transition out of the physical body.

Others, though, choose to end their beloved dog's suffering through euthanasia. This process is very much accepted in the compassionate care of animals.

Animals cannot express their wishes verbally or implement the mechanisms if their choice is euthanasia. It's up to you to do your best to hear through your heart what your dog wants, and to support him or her in the decision.

Having a veterinarian help ease Rexi's transition was one of the hardest decisions of my life. Rexi was my healing partner, companion, and friend, and I had shared twelve years of happiness with him. We did everything together. Our hearts were one. How could I make this seemingly final decision?

Yet, I saw how Rexi suffered, and it devastated me. I had come to know in my heart that an assisted passing was Rexi's wish and I was just helping to implement his soul's choice. And so, with overflowing love for Rexi, and feeling his love for me, I gave the final gift of a compassionate passing to my beloved companion and soul mate.

Nonetheless, for weeks afterwards I struggled with whether I had done what was right. Eventually I came to know in my heart that it took love and courage for me to trust in what I believed Rexi's soul was telling me.

I drew on my spiritual understanding and practices both in preparation for and after Rexi's passing. I encourage you to do the same, whatever that understanding and those practices may be.

In the room at my home in which I perform my healings, I placed a comfortable padded blanket in the doggie bed to comfort Rexi. I prepared the room with a sage cleansing, and lit incense and candles. I played the Tibetan singing bowls that Rexi loved to hear and that Buddhist monks often use in their meditations and rituals.

The day before Rexi was put to sleep,

we invited close friends and family to spend time with him and say goodbye. Although he had not eaten anything at all for an entire week, we got him a Whopper hamburger as a meal, something we had never done before. Rexi walked slowly to it, smelled it, and then devoured every morsel of this special final meal.

We had the veterinarian come to our house the next day. If feasible, I encourage you to do the same so your beloved animal transitions in familiar surroundings. I held and gently stroked Rexi, and through my heart sent love. I told Rexi over and over again how much I loved and appreciated him.

Although afterwards I did question whether I had done the right thing, at the time I was just present, and knew this was what Rexi's soul wanted and welcomed. I knew he was grateful that I was with him during his transition. I held him close and couldn't stop crying. Rexi left the Earth plane with grace and dignity. He knew it was time to say goodbye.

Other species seem to have a clearer understanding than humans of the right time to transition into the next stage of existence. They accept their passing as part of the natural cycle of the seasons of life, and they know life continues without a physical body. In this respect, and I believe in others as well, they understand life and spirituality at a more advanced level than many humans.

A common denominator among spiritual paths is the understanding that when our physical bodies die, our essences move from the world of form into the world of spirit. We miss the soft touch, the warmth, the sometimes messy but always loving licking, and the omnipresent companionship of our dogs. The connection, though, is eternal. Knowing this in your heart is a blessing and a source of great comfort.

The veterinarian left with Rexi's body so he could be cremated and his ashes returned to us. We still keep them in a special place in our home, along with those of Rocky.

In the evening I performed a shamanic ritual drawn from the ancient Incan "medicine wheel" tradition that honors the four directions and the elements of air, earth, water, and fire. At my altar, I lit candles, chanted, and prayed. I folded up a picture of Rexi and set it aflame, the smoke gently swirling upward. The ritual opened a gateway to the greater cosmos through which Rexi's spirit could pass.

It would take months for me to pass through the Five Stages of Grief, but performing the ritual made me feel lighter, at least for that night. The next morning, I noticed a shift in my consciousness, for I knew that Rexi was at peace on the Rainbow Bridge, and that when it becomes my turn to cross over to the light, he will be there to greet me.

Spiritual Practice
#3:

**Open yourself up to receive
messages from your beloved dog.**

Our angels in doggie form want to stay
connected to us after they pass into spirit,
and they let us know this through different
sensations and visual signs. The only
hurdles in communicating with them exist
within us, not them.

47

Some people don't believe in life after death. Others aren't sure, and question whether there is a Rainbow Bridge to heaven. Some may be frightened of the unknowns of death and cope with their fear by not thinking about existence in other dimensions.

Since before the dawn of civilization, however, people haven't just believed the spirit world exists, they've known it. Communication between the material and spiritual realms is a normal, everyday occurrence.

Doubt is the number one reason messages from the spirit world are missed. Don't doubt. Believe! Be open to the signs that your precious dog is present and letting you know that all is well. Our four-legged companions are still by our sides, and it is up to us to stay alert for the signs that they are with us.

Signs of the afterlife

Two days after Rexi's crossing, he gave me the first indication of his presence. I walked into my bathroom, felt chills in my body, and smelled a sweet aroma. I had not lit incense that day, and while the aroma had a hint of sandalwood, it was quite different from anything I had ever smelled—otherworldly, if you will.

Among the ways in which spirits communicate with us is through the sense of smell. Psychics call this "clairalience," or "clear scent." The spirit world through clairalience reconfirms that our loved ones are still with us, and I was certain Rexi was lying on the soft white carpet on which he always napped when I took a shower.

A few days later, I sat in the corner of the kitchen where I always gave Rexi his favorite treats, including the carrots and green beans he savored so much. *I miss us being together. We were a team*, I thought.

I soon noticed a fresh wind caressing my foot and felt the unmistakable sensation of Rexi's paw touching my leg. I knew his spirit was with me.

The most common type of contact with dogs that have crossed over into spirit is sensing their presence, as I did with Rexi. You might feel your dog next to you in bed or playing nearby as you work in the garden. You might ask yourself; *Did I just make that up? Did I really feel my dog in my bed?* That's natural. Know that the spirit world is real. If you have such a feeling, speak aloud and acknowledge to your beloved animal that you are aware of his or her presence.

Among the most important tools in getting in touch with the spirit world is simply to make a request. During your prayers or meditations, ask the Universe to send you signs of your dog's presence. If you stay attuned to your surroundings, you will be amazed at what happens. The signs may not come right away, but they will come.

I was taking a walk around my neighborhood five weeks after Rexi's passing, and felt saddened as I came to a favorite spot where we would stop so I could give him water and a treat. I looked at a sunset of beautiful orange, purple and blue, and although it had not rained, I saw in the sunset the Rainbow Bridge. This was the sign I had asked for, and I felt the gift of love that connects souls and binds us with our beloved animals forever.

Signs can come in many ways in nature. When a loved one passes, many people find cardinals showing up, their bright red feathers signaling that the spirit exists peacefully in another realm.

Does a butterfly keep appearing at your window? How about a hummingbird? These too can be signs of a beloved spirit's presence.

If you have other animal family members, pay attention to them. Do they often go to the place where their brother/sister slept? Do they bark or stare in one direction seemingly for no reason? Animals often can sense the presence of a spirit better than humans can.

The sky can bring messages. You may see in the clouds an image of your dog, or a spiritual symbol that connects you to the heavenly realm where your beloved animal dwells in peace and happiness.

Look for such synchronicities— "coincidences" with meaning. Don't be shocked when they appear, for they are a natural reflection of the interconnectedness of the cosmos.

Dreams, orbs, and visitations

"Why does the eye see a thing more clearly in dreams than the imagination when awake?"

So wrote Leonardo da Vinci, one of history's greatest geniuses.

When we are asleep in what is called the "REM" (rapid eye movement) state, we are in a place that links our earthly bodies to the spirit realm. The mind is not engaged in thinking or performing tasks, so it is open to otherworldly messages that come in the form of dreams.

Most animals communicate telepathically. They may appear playful in our dreams, which may be a sign that the time has come for us to lighten up a bit. Or, they may be licking a wound on our arm, showing us that we need to nurture ourselves in our time of grief.

53

Humans who are gifted animal intuitives are able to clearly see, hear, and receive insights from animals. I believe all of humankind is evolving towards this form of communication, and eventually everyone will converse with animals and other humans through a universal telepathic language.

We're generally more open to communication from our beloveds in the spirit world when we're asleep. Our animal companions show up in our dreams because they know how much we love and miss them. Dream visitations are an ideal way for them to contact you and contribute again to your happiness and sense of well-being.

Some of you may see globe-like objects called "spirit orbs." Most orbs appear in photographs, but for some people, including me, they also appear during meditation. Many psychics and healers say that orbs are from the spiritual realm and can signal the presence of angels or spirit guides.

Pay attention to the color of the orb. **GREEN** represents the heart center and unconditional love; **BLUE**, intuition, protection and communication; **YELLOW**, inner strength and transformation; **PINK**, forgiveness and healing; **PURPLE**, transcendent information and telepathic communication with angels and spirit guides; **SILVER**, attachment to beloved animals and humans; **GOLD**, infinite change and God's presence.

A few months after Rexi's passing, while meditating with my eyes closed just before falling asleep, I started seeing a bright, pulsating purple orb moving towards and away from me. I sensed in it Rexi's loving essence. I would open my eyes and the orb would still be there. Night after night the orb would appear. I would thank Rexi for bringing me comfort and fall into a deep and restful sleep.

Eventually the purple orb turned into an image of Rexi exactly as I remembered him. When I opened my eyes, the image remained. When I closed them again, a bright golden glow appeared around Rexi that soon changed to purple and then to an angelic white. This happened nightly for a couple of months, and each time I would start sobbing and telling Rexi how much I loved him. As the sobbing passed, the image would disappear, and I'd feel a sense of deep inner peace.

Then one night, to my amazement, a human male appeared like a hologram in place of Rexi. His three-dimensional image was surrounded in an aura of brightly pulsating colors encompassing the entire spectrum.

He appeared as both form and energy simultaneously. The gaze of his deep-set eyes mesmerized me, and I felt as if I were floating in the darkness of the Universe surrounded by a trillion stars. My breathing slowed. Time and the material world did not exist, and I found myself at one with unconditional love.

The wisdom of the ages exuded from the countenance of this celestial being. He did not give me his name, but I sensed I was in the presence of what many people call an "Ascended Master."

Through thought he said to me: "You know this is not my only form, for I exist as a timeless and infinite spirit. I have been with you many lifetimes and shall ever be guiding you. For now, all you have to know is that we have work to do together."

I was surprised by the appearance of this spirit guide, but not shocked. We all have spirit guides, and some of us are fortunate enough to see them when they communicate with us.

His words, "We have work to do together,"

had a profound impact on me. I had experienced months of sadness and anger as I progressed through the Five Stages of Grief, but now I knew I had to move forward. What is the "work" the spirit guide mentioned? I'm not completely certain, but as time progressed, I realized part of it was to write this book.

Spiritual Practice #4:

Reach out for holistic healing support.

Dealing with the passing of a beloved animal can be intensely painful. The emotions we feel, particularly the anger of the second stage of grief, can even cause physical pain and illness. The loss affects our body, mind, and spirit, and it's easier to move through the grief when we adopt a holistic approach to the healing process.

Here are a few suggestions that helped me:

- Don't be afraid to ask for help from friends and relatives. Call or meet with people who will listen to your stories of your beloved dog and empathize with you. This type of support is vital.

Those in grief don't necessarily need advice, but they do need to be heard, and talking about your grief is one of the best therapies.

- Contact with nature fills the soul and the senses. We hear the birds sing, the frogs croak and the crickets chirp. We smell the flowers, feel the coolness of the shade trees and the warmth of the sun. We hear the wind blowing through the trees and the soothing sound of flowing water in a creek, or the roar of ocean surf. Regardless of one's spiritual or religious beliefs, being in nature nourishes the soul.

- Exercise helps greatly. When you are grieving over the loss of your dog, depression can make it hard to climb out of bed or get out of the chair. Make the effort. Swimming, bicycling, running or brisk walking releases hormones in the brain called endorphins, which can give us a sense of well-being

- I used to teach hatha yoga, and I can't say enough about the physical and spiritual benefits of the practice. For dealing with your grief, I recommend taking hatha yoga classes.

- The ancient Chinese healing art of acupuncture can relieve pain and get what the Chinese call "qi" flowing through the body's energy channels. Massage therapy, Reiki, healing touch and numerous other modalities also can help move energy, relieve pain, and enhance your well-being.

Connecting with spirit through meditation

Although it was weeks after Rexi's passing before I could again meditate, of all the practices in dealing with grief, meditation for me turned out to be the most important. This is why I am giving it a section all its own.

Meditation has been taught throughout the ages by gurus and saints from all spiritual paths, and today even Western medicine has begun to acknowledge the health benefits of meditating. It can reduce stress, lower blood pressure, and even boost the immune system.

Most of all, by quieting the mind through regular meditation, we can gain an understanding through direct experience of the Oneness of creation and our own Divine nature.

I've taught meditation for many years and often have heard people tell me they can't meditate because the chatter in their mind is too great. But chatter exists in everyone's mind—even people who have meditated for decades. It's impossible to completely shut off our thoughts, but there are techniques that can slow our thinking and help us to look not without, but within.

The first thing to do is find a place where you will not be disturbed. Some people have altars in their homes. If you do, consider sitting in front of it as you meditate. Great yogis often are pictured seated in the "full lotus" position, with each foot resting on the opposite thigh. Don't worry if you can't sit like this. It's fine to just sit cross-legged or in a chair with your spine straight, your hands on your thighs or one atop the other in your lap.

One approach that I use often is "candle gazing." In a darkened room, look indirectly at a flickering candle. You may begin to see the flow of energy between you and the candle as you become deeply relaxed.

Candle gazing can open a portal that awakens you to the reality of etheric realms. Just gently close your eyes and visualize the candle at the place between your eyebrows known as your "third eye." Gently open your eyes again and see the physical candle. By going back and forth, you can ride the wave between this and other dimensions.

In my classes, we often do candle gazing with many candles in the middle of a group circle. People who previously were frustrated with meditation often find this opens things up for them, enabling them to appreciate the benefits of meditation for the first time.

Some people prefer to meditate in silence, others with soothing music. You might also consider playing a recording of a tamboura, an East Indian string instrument that produces a deeply calming background sound. Experiment to see what's right for you.

It's good to start with several deep yogic breaths. Breathe in through your nose to a count of four. Hold for a count of two, then breathe out through the nose for a count of four.

You might also want to start your meditation by chanting a mantra, generally a Sanskrit syllable or words with a mystical significance that help instill one-pointed concentration. I wrote earlier about the mantra I often use, *Om Namah Shivaya*. Another popular mantra is *So-Ham*, with *So* chanted on the in-breath and *Ham* on the out-breath. It means "I am that." Mantras can be spoken aloud or chanted mentally.

After the mantra, strive to still your mind and just watch your thoughts as they come and go. If the mind wanders too far, bring it back by again saying the mantra or counting your breaths for a time.

Eventually, as your meditations deepen, you may find that your breath deepens and slows. You may even start to feel heavier. At some point, though, you may feel you have no breath as you find yourself suspended in a place of pure consciousness. None of this is very complicated, unusual or "out there." The mystical experiences that result from meditation happen when you cease seeking them and just let yourself BE.

You might also consider creating a ritual as part of your meditation. It could be as simple as lighting a candle and striking a gong at the beginning, and blowing out the candle and again striking the gong at the end.

Just before and after meditation is a good time to pray. Consider asking for a sign that your beloved animal is with you. In your meditation you might even find that you can sense his or her presence.

Spiritual growth

In Eastern spiritual traditions there's a wonderful concept called "dharma." There are nuanced differences in its meaning among the great Eastern religions, but in general, dharma points towards a higher truth, a universal law, that pervades the Universe.

I believe souls incarnate on Earth for a purpose and to learn lessons and move towards a greater understanding of that higher truth. The incarnations happen again and again, enabling us to progress, or regress, in our spiritual understanding.

As we pass through the Five Stages of Grief, it sometimes can be hard to realize we are learning important lessons that help us to better understand ourselves and our place in the cosmos. By gaining this wisdom, we are able to live nobler and more fulfilling lives. It's only after we have reached the Acceptance stage of grief that we can look back and fully appreciate the lessons we have learned and the progress we have made.

In dealing with my grief, I learned to truly understand the constantly changing nature of material forms—and the eternal nature of the soul. My beloved Rexi's physical form passed from the material world, but Rexi continues to support and love me from the realm of eternal spirit. I know this because I can feel his love as I go through each day.

Dealing with grief also taught me patience. Sometimes it seemed my sadness and depression would remain with me forever, but ever so gradually I began to feel tinges of well-being. Sometimes I would slip back a bit, but I could tell the general direction was towards a reopening of my heart.

During my grief I learned how to count my joys and blessings. I had lost Rexi, but he had given me so much love and happiness, and those memories would always be with me.

A breakthrough came when I stopped resisting my feelings of anger, sadness and frustration, and began observing my thoughts from the perspective of the "witness"—the immortal part of me. I no longer was attached to my thoughts, and understood that even in grief I was in harmony with the Universe.

The Universe will tell you much if you pay attention to it and its angelic messengers. One way it communicates is with sequences of numbers, often referred to as "angel numbers." The sequences may show up on a digital clock, a check, a license plate, or in countless other ways.

1-1-1 tells you that you are at a place in life where you should slow down, take a well-deserved break, and learn how to "smell the roses." It symbolizes the unconditional love of the "Divine Feminine." People often say they smell roses when they sense the presence of Mother Mary. The numerical sequence also symbolizes Gaia, or Mother Earth.

2-2-2 informs us that our lives have fallen out of balance and we need to take steps to restore equilibrium. The philosophers of ancient China spoke of yin and yang, forces that appear as opposites but actually interconnect, complement, and give rise to each other. Pay attention when this numerical sequence knocks on your door, for it tells you that something in your life is amiss.

3-3-3 is the angels' way of assuring us that we are doing well, we are on the right track, and we are stronger than we may think. In sacred geometry, the number 3 manifests as a triangle and tells us that our lives are in balance. Picture the two mirror images of the number 3. Viewed together, they resemble the symbol for infinity. When I finish a Reiki session, I trace the symbol in the air with my arm, showing the ever-flowing nature of infinite energy and intelligence.

Whatever numbers show up, always remember that you are Divine, you are the Source, and you are one with the Creator.

Spiritual Practice #5:

Let God in.

Opening our hearts to animal soul mates and companions is one of life's greatest joys. Are these beloved family members literally angels (or in the case of some, actually Ascended Masters) sent specifically to help us experience joy and unconditional love, and maybe teach us a few lessons our souls need to learn? Remember when the animal intuitive talked with Rocky and Rocky said he had work to do from the "other side," and when a being with the aura of an Ascended Master appeared to me in place of Rexi?

Whether literally or metaphorically angelic, the lives of these angels in doggie bodies are short compared to the human lifespan.

We enter into a relationship with them knowing that, in all probability, they will pass into spirit well before we do, and we may experience intense grief when their physical bodies leave us.

Yet, the joy they bring is so great that most of the time we eventually open our hearts again and let another beloved animal into our lives. The joy stems from love—our love for them, and their love for us. It is a pure, unconditional love without expectations. It is God's love—and God is Love.

The French poet and novelist Anatole France seems to have understood this when he wrote, "Until one has loved an animal, a part of one's soul remains unawakened."

I certainly can relate to France's sentiments. Perhaps you can as well. Through both their lives and their passing, our beloved animals teach us about love, and about ourselves.

Duality and unity

The material world into which we've been born causes us to perceive opposites. There's light and dark, good and evil, pain and pleasure, wet and dry. In this dualistic framework, our emotions are like the positive and negative poles of a magnet. It often seems one cannot exist without the other.

Throughout the millennia, however, many sages have taught that this world of duality is an illusion, and that it is possible to go beyond perceived duality into a state of consciousness where everything is part of a Divine Oneness. In spiritual circles today, you will hear people say, "We are all One." I believe that is true, but what does it mean?

Perhaps we can get a deeper insight into the meaning by looking at the concept of Mother Gaia.

In ancient Greece, the goddess Gaia was the personification of Mother Earth. Today, her name is applied to the idea that Earth is a single organism and we are a part of it. Just as a single blood cell coursing through our body is an integral part of us, we are a cell in Gaia. Similarly, Gaia is a cell in an infinite and interconnected cosmos.

Sages also have taught that Earth is the plane on which we can awaken and learn there is no separation between "I" and "the other," and that although we do not always see it, the cosmos is governed by Love, Light and Truth—the magnificent energy of the Divine.

Learning to live in this Oneness can open a portal to ascension. When we feel in the depths of our souls, "I am you and you are I," somehow everything shifts.

Know that there is a state of grace that surrounds all of us. It is loving and eternal. The light of grace re-establishes within us the wisdom to recognize "Oneness"—the singular essence of all that is.

Grief can morph into hope

The passing of Rexi and the grief that hurt so much caused me to look more deeply within than I ever had. This enabled me to understand through my mind, but also through my heart, some great truths:

- Nothing in the Universe is more natural than the flow of joy and inspiration.

- Our souls connect with the entire Universe, which is the source of inspiration and creative power.

- The material world constantly changes, but love is constant and eternal. Love is the source of all joy.

- Once we allow our hearts to expand, we will find ourselves coming into harmony with Universal Truth. It is then that the lessons of the Universe will begin to unfold.

The sorrow that humans so often feel stems from their imagined separation from God, but nothing exists in the material world that is not Godly. The Creator never leaves us. If you are experiencing sorrow, breathe in God's presence.

Trust God fully, for God will give you the love and strength you need to pass through the stages of grief. God will teach you how to open your heart again to joy by recognizing the Divine essence within you.

When you again feel a touch of joy, take time to be present with it. All is Divine perfection. You are doing amazingly well exactly where you are.

Spiritual Practice #6:

Stand tall in your truth.

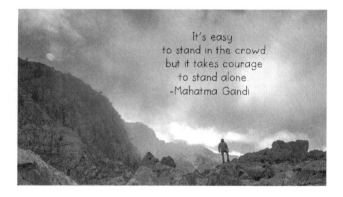

It's easy
to stand in the crowd
but it takes courage
to stand alone.
-Mahatma Gandi

One of my favorite places is Sedona, Arizona, halfway between Phoenix and the Grand Canyon. It had been six months since Rexi's transition, and while I had not passed fully through the Five Stages of Grief, I felt energized enough to follow my inner guidance and visit this sacred area again.

Sedona is known for its majestic, red, rocky landscape, sculpted by the elements over the eons. It has been said that God made the Grand Canyon but dwells in Sedona.

There's a spiritual, transcendent atmosphere in the "red rock country" and its environs. For the original native population, it has been a sacred place for millennia. Today it is a pilgrimage site for people from around the world who seek spiritual understanding.

Along with its physical majesty, Sedona is known for its invisible vortexes—swirling centers of energy that facilitate healing, deep meditation, self-exploration, and even contact with unseen worlds. I had come across vortexes in previous visits and found them alive with surging energy.

Two months before Rexi's passing, I had bought an amulet representing the goddess Isis, one of the most beloved deities of ancient Egypt. She is a goddess of healing and an expression of Divine love.

The talisman of gold, silver, ruby-like tourmaline and other stones was not a physical image of Isis. It represented her powers and featured the intersecting tetrahedrons of the *Merkaba*, an ancient sacred geometric design that assists people in expanding their consciousness, experiencing angelic realms, and even traveling through time. I made sure to wear the talisman around my neck on a leather cord during my entire visit to Sedona.

The far, far distant past

A few days after my arrival, I set out to explore the area's spiritual wonders.

I had hired my guide some weeks before I arrived because he had an excellent reputation for knowing the exact location of the vortexes. Middle-aged and quite fit, he was a sturdy hiker who knew Sedona well. Our spiritual natures were different, but I sought only directions to sacred places, not spiritual advice.

We hiked first to a spot where three majestic trees stood amid the red rocks, their branches reaching out to one another as if they were holding hands. Three trees together often show the presence of a vortex, and this one, I soon discovered, was quite powerful.

I sat on a rock by the trees, whose shade provided some comfort from Sedona's dry September heat. With the Isis talisman around my neck, I closed my eyes and soon found myself transported through a tunnel into another time and place.

I saw an image of elderly women wearing white linen dresses, their shoulders covered with shawls or mantels. Black or green cosmetics highlighted their eyes, and they were adorned with black braided wigs, necklaces and bracelets of copper, gold, turquoise and other fine stones. I sensed they were the wise women of this mystical realm.

Suddenly I felt an electrical current rising through my spine, then spreading outward, filling my whole body. I began shaking from head to toe. As the shaking settled, I found myself in what I recognized as an ancient Egyptian temple. Huge columns with brightly painted carvings of gods and goddesses held up the ceiling. Incense burned in cauldrons, its sweet and soothing smell spreading throughout the temple as the sound of chanting reverberated off the walls.

Before me was the god Anubis, with the body of a man and the head of a jackal, standing by a coffin. Anubis, a god of the underworld who presides over rituals for the dead, is not a gruesome or frightening figure. Yes, he deals with death. But is not death part of the natural cycle of life, death, and rebirth?

Near me stood the beautiful goddess Isis, whose love for humanity knows no bounds. She was dressed in white and wore a headdress with the sun disc resting between two antelope horns. She had revivified her murdered husband, Osiris, and served as the goddess of resurrection and renewal.

As I stood in this majestic setting, I realized I was being initiated as a priestess and a healer who would study the ancient healing arts. I also understood that I would learn secrets so I might look not only through my own eyes, but also through the mystical, all-seeing and all-knowing eye of Isis' son, Horus, the god of order. Horus had lost an eye in battle, but Thoth, the god of wisdom, restored it through his healing magic.

I wished to stay in this majestic setting longer. Indeed, I felt I could stay forever.

But then I heard the soft voice of my guide: "Ishwari. It is time for you to return." Slowly my consciousness came back to the present.

"I have never seen anything like it," the guide told me. "Your face changed in appearance, particularly your eyes, and I sensed around you the energy of Isis."

The guide's comment did not surprise me. It confirmed to me that my consciousness for a time had existed in a fifth, sixth, or even tenth dimension.

I had been granted a glimpse of a past life, but realized it also reflected parts of my present life. In my grief over the death of my beloved Rexi, I had experienced the depths of my shadow side. As a result, I had many insights. In an emotional sense, I had gone through a death and resurrection, and do not Anubis and Isis represent those same things?

In this life, too, I am a healer, just as I was millennia ago. Perhaps you can relate to my story and recognize that the lives we live today are built on the many lives we lived before.

The inner child

My guide led me to a second vortex not far away. Again, three trees marked the spot. I sat on a rock, closed my eyes, and soon found myself standing in a green field, looking at a playful girl in the distance. She was about twelve, with long brown hair and bangs, and dressed in white bell-bottom pants and a sleeveless white top.

The girl ran up to me, and I realized I was looking at myself when I was her age. We embraced. "Don't ever push me away again," she said. "I love you. Don't be angry or sad. Open the door to your heart and let me in."

Those words caused me to realize how deeply sad and angry I was because of Rexi's death. But soon my heart opened as I—and my inner child—hugged each other and became one. In this sublime state I heard birds singing. When my inner child and I separated and I opened my eyes, the bird songs became louder, as if a celestial choir had broken out in Divine harmony.

This brought a smile to my lips, for it confirmed the angelic realm had been involved in passing on the wisdom that had just been given me. As we grow older, we so often lose touch with our childlike nature. What a shame, for it is in this nature that we find true joy, unsullied by the trials and stresses of the adult world.

If you are deep in grief because of a loss, I encourage you to embrace your inner child. Perhaps you should look at pictures of yourself during a happy childhood event, then meditate and try to return to that carefree time. The inner child helps us open our hearts and again embrace the joys of life.

Eternal love

It had been a long and eventful day, but my guide insisted we visit one more vortex, for he sensed it would be of great benefit to me.

We hiked to a beautiful, shaded ravine. I sat on a rock, took off my hiking boots and socks, and felt the soothing energy of the rocks on my feet. I looked up at the majestic blue sky and trees, yet felt sadness as I thought of Rexi.

I closed my eyes and sat for a time in meditation, but sensed nothing special about this site. *What was the guide talking about? There's no vortex here*, I thought.

Soon, however, I felt a swirling sensation. *The wind?* No. The energy was too compact and intense. The swirling increased and I knew I was in the vortex, which transported me into another realm and opened a tunnel through which I gazed. In the distance I saw a speck coming toward me, and as it got closer I saw it was a sturdy, fawn-white dog with pointy ears running as fast as he could.

Yes, it was Rexi, and my heart jumped with joy as my beloved companion leapt into my lap with unbounded energy and began licking my face, just as he had done so many times on the earthly plane. Rexi's form was much more than a vision, for I felt his weight against my body and the wetness of his tongue on my skin.

I knew Rexi was of the spirit realm and our visit would be brief, for I would have to return to the earthly world. In the moments we spent together, though, we shared limitless joy.

I hugged my beloved Rexi, and he spoke to me through thought: "Do not despair.

Find joy in life as a child finds joy. We have been together always, in different forms but also formless, and we will be together throughout eternity."

For me this was a turning point. Rexi's form dissolved back into the ethereal realm, but I now knew there was no reason to despair, for he would be with me always. Rexi's appearance pulled some key points of my life together. Through his playfulness while in the material world, he had enabled me to be childlike. I had on this day embraced my twelve-year-old self, and with Rexi's visit as spirit, the healing of my inner child finally felt complete.

As I walked back towards town with the guide, I pondered the day's events—among the most profound of my life.

I knew intuitively that the Divine singing of the birds was a sign from the spirit world of protection and support as I regained my power in the Mother Earth energy of

Sedona. My time in the Egyptian temple showed me that I had made the right choice when I became a healer—no doubt a choice I had made in many different lifetimes. The meeting between me as an adult and me as a young girl showed that although we age, we must always strive to maintain childlike joy.

I had tried so hard to hang onto Rexi, but because of our brief visit at the third vortex I understood now that it was time to let go of my attachment to grief. *All is in Divine order; everything is part of the Creator.* I felt grounded again in my body and joy in learning even more deeply how to walk and talk my truth.

Beyond the beyond

The events of my first day's foray into Sedona's spiritual energies were profound, and I wondered what events lay in store for me on my second adventure. Could they possibly be as momentous?

My guide this time was Anahata, which is also the Sanskrit name for the "heart chakra," the spinning vortex in the center of the chest that connects us to the love and compassion of the Universe. The name fit perfectly. When we met at the home of a friend with whom I was staying, she placed her hand on my high heart. As I looked into the blue eyes of this beautiful woman, I felt the warmth of peaceful love from her heart. I felt a soul connection and sensed that our meeting was not by chance.

At my request, we went first to Peace Park, a site at the base of the imposing

Thunder Mountain. We left the car nearby and hiked up a stony path. Buddhist prayer flags attached to the pinyon and juniper pines waved in a gentle breeze, and the tinkling of wind chimes enhanced the mystical aura of this sacred site. I had been to Peace Park in previous visits to Sedona and found it inspiring, but this time I somehow knew the visit would be special.

The path ended at an open area dominated by a stupa three-and-a-half stories high and dedicated to Buddha Amitabha— the "Buddha of Limitless Light." In the Buddhist tradition, stupas serve as storehouses for relics and offerings and as places for prayers and meditation. The rectangular base terraced upwards to a dome with a pinnacle on top from which lines of colorful prayer flags stretched to the ground. The reddish color of the stupa blended perfectly with the red rocks of magical Sedona.

I found myself drawn to a large wooden carving of the Buddha. He was seated in the lotus position, right arm raised and left arm resting on his lap. Both hands had the thumb and forefinger touching in *chin mudra*, a gesture of knowledge and wisdom.

I began walking clockwise around the statue chanting the ancient Sanskrit mantra *Om Mane Padme Hum*. The words translate as "Praise to the jewel in the lotus," but the literal meaning was not important. The mantra's power came from its vibration, which transported me to a peaceful realm where I felt in every cell of my body the Universal love and compassion expressed by the Buddha for all sentient beings that are suffering.

I'm not sure how long I circled the statue, for I had lost all track of time, but after a while I walked over to my guide and sat with her on a bench near the stupa. I closed my eyes and felt the swirling energy of a vortex. I had no awareness of my body, for my consciousness had expanded beyond the person known as Ishwari and merged with the infinite consciousness of the cosmos.

The yoga masters call this state *samadhi*. While in it, the perception of duality that creates the illusion of the material world vanishes.

My consciousness had pierced the veil of illusion and become one with all things as it floated in a sea of Universal love. In this sublime state I understood we are not here to judge the events that take place in our lives, for they are all part of the infinite play of Universal consciousness and linked in a web that reaches to the distant stars.

At the moment of this realization, I found peace again after months of sadness and despair.

Anahata knew I had entered a most profound mystical state and the sense of time and place did not exist for me. She did not say a word or make any motion that I could detect, but I am certain that through her love and compassion she had supported me on my journey.

When my consciousness returned to my body, she told me I had been gone for at least forty minutes, though it could have been eternity as far as I was aware. She asked if I wanted to hike to the top of Thunder Mountain, but I told her I would rather take a short hike and find a secluded place to rest, contemplate, and ground myself to Mother Earth.

We walked from the park and off the trail to a spot with several flat red rocks shaded by trees. On one of the rocks, Anahata laid out a mesa cloth, a colorful fabric used on altars for many centuries by shamans throughout the Americas. She set upon it crystals, essential oils, sage, and a deck of shamanic oracle cards containing images of animals in nature. Together we prayed and sprinkled a few pinches of tobacco on the ground as an offering to the natural world around us.

I lay on a rock and looked at the cloudless blue sky through the branches of a pine tree, enjoying the coolness of the shade and the singing of a bird nearby. Anahata, an intuitive channel, asked if I would like to hear messages she was receiving from the spirit world.

I said yes, I would, and the spirits said I had a time of great joy and creativity ahead of me.

Afterwards I drew a card from the shamanic oracle deck on the altar. It was of a flying blue jay, symbolic of clarity and vision, tenacity, and the truth within one's heart. I took this as confirmation from the spirit world that it was time for me to renew with great vigor my shamanic calling as a spiritual healer.

We lovingly dismantled the altar and left, but soon I came upon a large feather in the middle of the trail. Is it from a bird, or an angel? I asked myself as I stooped to pick it up. Regardless, the message to me from the spirit world was clear: "You are on the right path."

Before returning to the car, we stopped at a nearby medicine wheel made from rocks placed on the dry earth. To the indigenous peoples, medicine wheels signify the cyclical patterns found in the cosmos and in life. Spokes reached out in the four directions, and as I walked around the medicine wheel I contemplated their meaning.

North, the direction in which a compass points, told me I needed to reassert my true essence and walk my true path as a healer. In the east, the direction of the rising sun, I saw a butterfly, which told me it was time to emerge from my chrysalis and renew my passion for life. Looking south, I saw a hummingbird drawing nectar from a flower, which told me I needed once more to taste the sweetness of life and be joyful and playful. Facing west, I pictured the setting sun and knew it was time to let my grief disappear below the horizon.

I felt great humility, and immense appreciation for the shamans whose connection with nature enabled them to conceive the medicine wheel. They were Native Americans, but shamans from many different cultures connect closely with nature and glean from it a spiritual understanding that has been all but lost in the modern world.

Spiritual Practice
#7:

Allow yourself to open to empowerment.

The beauty
you see in me
is a reflection
of you.
-Rumi

I believe our souls come to Earth with a Divine Plan, and once we remember who we truly are and align ourselves with carrying out that plan, the gift of well-being will be a constant in our lives.

Well-being does not necessarily include material wealth. It often does not. In the material realm, people can become attached to physical things that give instant but not lasting gratification. In their pursuit of more and more possessions, they may fail to develop close relationships with family and friends, and even abandon accepted moral and ethical standards.

But they won't be taking the objects of this world with them when they pass on to another dimension. There's nothing wrong with physical comforts and financial abundance, but if one's sole aim is to pursue happiness in the present moment through material possessions, one is not likely to live a fulfilling life.

I'm particularly fond of a quote by the poet Karen Ravn: "Only as high as I reach can I grow, only as far as I seek can I go;

only as deep as I look can I see, only as much as I dream can I be."

From my perspective, I also would say, "Only to the degree I can remove material illusion from my vision can I sense the joy of spiritual realms."

This is a message I share with my students, though sometimes I meet resistance. "Ishwari," some tell me, "you are different. When you meditate you travel to spiritual places that most people will never experience."

They often are surprised when I tell them that twenty-five years ago, I found my mind too full of chatter and my focus too worldly to meditate at all. Yes, I taught hatha yoga, but I concentrated on the physical positions and movements of my students, not on the spiritual aspect of yoga that serves as its true foundation.

One day, however, an artist friend who

expressed spiritual mysteries in her paintings suggested we meditate together with a recording of etheric music playing softly in the background. I don't know what was different, but I soon fell into a trance-like state in which I lost all sense of time.

At one point I found myself curled up in my mother's womb, aware that I had not yet been born into my current lifetime. I also experienced my consciousness floating in outer space. As I looked down at Earth, I was struck by the suffering of so many people and animals for whom our fragile planet is home. It was at this point the message came to me that I must do my part to help ease the suffering by becoming a spiritual teacher and healer.

I stayed in the trance for two hours, and the experience changed my life. Fortunately, my artist friend recognized what was happening and did not interfere.

Since then, I have opened my heart more and more to the spirit world, although, as I have related, I closed it for a time after the passing of my beloved Rexi. My visit to Sedona, however, reinforced in me the understanding that life is a great adventure, and that the spirit world will always guide me back to my true essence if I let it.

We all have our place in this magnificent Universe. We learn more about what that place is as we progress in age, experience, and knowledge. In this lifetime, as in past lifetimes, I have chosen to embrace the priestess in me. My destiny is to serve as a spiritual conduit, and to convey to others the truths of the Divine through my words and actions.

My spiritual name is Ishwari, but that is but a fraction of my being. I, like you and everyone else, am a part of a limitless consciousness that knows no bounds of time and space. I gained an understanding of this consciousness through direct experience and am striving to let you know you can experience that understanding too.

We are multidimensional beings who are not tied to a mundane material existence. In reality, our energy bodies are free to travel to other dimensions. To do so, however, we must overcome our fear of venturing into the unknown. Much has been revealed in the past century about the beings, known as Ascended Masters, who have attained an exalted spiritual state. We all are capable of such attainment, but to get there we must be willing to take that first step, as they did millennia ago.

We can look at our beloved doggies and realize that so many are farther along in their spiritual ascension than most humans, for they are able to show us what unconditional love is all about.

We are learning again the age-old truth that we attract into our lives that which we focus on. People who talk constantly about their suffering attract more suffering. Conversely, if they focus on joy, they ride a wave of joy. If we think of love and act with love in our hearts, our love will expand to others and we will help the entire world ascend to a perfect state of loving consciousness.

Change is constant, and we never know what change the next day, or even the next hour, will bring. For me, my awakening to the spiritual realms came rapidly. For most, it comes more slowly—but it will come if you look for messages from the spirit world and follow them wherever they might lead.

Here are a few principles to consider living by as you seek spiritual understanding:

- Embrace life as the hero of your own story.
- When you are afraid to jump into the unknown—JUMP!

- Follow your instincts and creative impulses.
- Change is your friend. Clarity is your power.
- Great challenges present great opportunities.
- Enthusiasm for service to humanity is a gift from the Divine.

Happy holidays

At Christmastime in 2019, my husband, Moises, and I were dining outside at a Mexican restaurant, enjoying both the food and the cool South Florida weather. Out of the blue, my husband suggested we stop by a shop that worked with accomplished dog breeders and look at the puppies

The shop was open late that evening, and with a touch of anxiety I agreed. I had been to the shop some months before, but the memory of Rexi had caused me to break down in tears. I had not yet passed sufficiently through the Five Stages of Grief to be able to handle such close contact with the playful and loving puppies without longing for Rexi.

This visit, however, was different. I had reached the Acceptance stage of grief, and I knew Rexi's spirit wanted me to move on with my life.

Moises and I had petted a few puppies when the owner mentioned he had a French bulldog—a "blue"—in the back of the shop that had just arrived the day before. "Blue" is one of the colors of Frenchies, although it actually is more a shade of gray.

When the owner returned with this six-pound cutie, my heart jumped with joy. My husband and I couldn't let go of him. We petted him and rubbed his belly. He responded with licks to our faces and hands, and both of us wondered whether we should take him home.

Inviting a puppy into one's life is not a decision to be taken lightly. We would be embarking on a serious relationship that would last for many years, so Moises and I decided to discuss the matter further and sleep on it.

We had been planning to take a cruise, but having a new puppy requires a lot of time and energy. We'd need to bond with him, train him, nurture him, and show him he could trust us. Getting a puppy and leaving on a cruise just aren't compatible.

A cruise or a dog? The choice turned out to be easy: the puppy!

Early the next morning I called the manager and told him to hold onto the little Frenchie and that I'd be there shortly to pick him up.

We named the puppy Magu, which is far

from a common name. But I have a little secret to tell you. With but one letter change, Magu becomes Mago, which in my native language, Spanish, means "Wizard."

A bundle of joy

The thirteenth-century Sufi poet and mystic Rumi tells us, "Don't you know yet? It is your light that lights the world."

That light shines brightest when we're feeling joy, and joy surfaces most strongly when our hearts and souls unite. This union is achieved when we are proceeding along our Divine Path and understand that whatever happens to us, that path leads to our highest good.

When we pass through the Five Stages of Grief, joy may seem but a distant memory. But even in our darkest hours, if we persist in striving to open ourselves to light and love, eventually we again will find joy in our lives.

Magu is a bundle of joy. When I'm with him in public, he attracts children like the nectar of a flower attracts hummingbirds and bees. The children reach out to him to play, and he responds with unbridled joyful energy. They all caress him while Magu kisses them back.

Magu has not replaced Rexi. That would be impossible. The love and experiences Rexi and I shared were unique. Magu has instead followed Rexi into my life. He brings his own spirit with him, and together we are having our own experiences that will help our spirits to blossom. As Rexi assisted in my growth, so will Magu, though perhaps in different ways.

Rexi still visits me from time to time in my dreams and meditations, and I'm sure he always will. The bond between us will never be broken. But I knew even before the arrival of Magu that the time had come for Rexi's spirit to move on so he could guide others, as well as me, from his transcendent home.

Rely on your inner strength to ensure your dreams are realized

The moment we say, "I want, I choose, I allow," the non-physical part of our being in concert with the Universe begins manifesting our desires. When we are in despair, however, these words can be hard, or even impossible, to speak.

I had to pass through the stages of grief before I was able to say the words, but when I finally did, I experienced a great sense of empowerment. I began to see with even greater clarity what is expected of me as a healer and an intuitive.

Among other things, I knew I needed to write this book with the hope and expectation that it would help others respond to the loss of their four-legged soul mates in a way that might enable them to grow spiritually and move on to the next empowered stage of their lives.

When we set our intention and open ourselves to its guidance, the Universe will deliver us the experiences, people and resources to help us achieve our goals. You have only to ask with love and conviction and the Universe will play its part.

The Universe brought Rexi into my life. I experienced joy because of Rexi, but also, later, despair. In the material world of duality, where all emotions have their opposites, we can't experience one without the other.

My beloved Rexi can serve as an example to all of us about the source of true happiness, for he possessed "dog energy" in abundance. That energy constantly reminds us to be loyal and truthful to ourselves—and to those around us.

NAMASTE
*I salute the Divine
at the center of your being.*

Acknowledgments

I bow to the Creator for giving me the inspiration for this book, and the strength needed to write it so I could help others heal from grief and advance along their spiritual paths.

There are no words to express the deepest soul connection I have with my husband. In our forty-three years of marriage, you continue to provide the space for me to express my true Divine self always. You support and love me unconditionally. I love you.

To Lynn S. Bachrach, president of ttlharmony Publishing, what can I say? Lynn, you are an answer to my prayers. First, thank you for believing in me and my spiritual guidance. The scope of support that you and your best-in-class team provide means everything to me.

This book, and the quality and presence of it, would just be a sparkle in my eye without you and your team. I love you.

A special shout-out to the world's best Senior Editor, Kingsley Guy. Infinite thanks for your brilliance in making this diamond shine. I am forever grateful.

Susan Szecsi—you are simply the very best there is! Your artistic talents bowl me over, you know book design better than anyone and your judgment, wisdom and beautiful heart add depth and balance to everything you touch. I'm honored to have you brighten the artistic presentation of my book. Thank you, I love you.

With awe and eternal love to the talented Luciana Guerra for seeing in meditation the image of Rexi's energy exactly as he came to me in Sedona and having the artistic talent to capture this perfectly with the cover artwork. Namaste.

About the Author

Ishwari *(Rina Lichtinger)* is a lightworker and author who supports people's awakening to their Divine plans.

A compassionate ordained minister and a clairvoyant, Ishwari for the past twenty-five years has channeled Divine healing energy, resulting in deep physical, emotional and spiritual transformations for more than thirteen thousand clients.

During this time, she has been a leading spiritual and advanced yoga and meditation teacher for a loyal following and has earned the Experienced Registered Yoga Teacher 500 (E-RYT 500) recognition.

The American Cancer Society in 2000 honored Rina Lichtinger as "Woman of the Year" for her commitment to helping abused children, which included raising $250,000 for this important cause.

The Fort Lauderdale Philharmonic Society recognized Rina Lichtinger as a "Woman of Substance and Style," and Bank of America and *Latina Style* magazine recognized her with the "Hispanic Woman of Distinction Award."

Ishwari has been featured on television, including Channel 10 News in Fort

Lauderdale; Channel 17 with the late Steven Goldstein, host of "We the People"; with Ana Maria Polo, host of "Caso Cerrado"; and with Francis Helen, host of "Dimension Desconocida."

Ishwari through her writing now shares her inspirational stories and messages with a broader audience. Along with *Paws of Love*, she is also the author of the highly praised spiritually channeled books *Visions of Light* and *The Enchanted Land—A Healing Story for Children.*

A respected spiritual leader in her South Florida community, Rina Lichtinger was given the Sanskrit name "Ishwari" by the late, widely acclaimed yogi Mukunda Stiles. The name reflects an encompassing, compassionate, powerful goddess energy.

Your Divine Plan

Helping people awaken to their Divine plans™

www.yourdivineplan.net

Ishwari@yourdivineplan.net

YOUR DIVINE PLAN